in her own words

Marilyn Monroe

Guus Luijters

OMNIBUS PRESS
LONDON · NEW YORK · SYDNEY

Format designed by Ranch Associates
Art direction by Mike Bell
Cover designed by Liz Nicholson

ISBN 0.7119.2302.7
Order No. OP 46010

Exclusive distributors:

Book Sales Limited,
8/9 Frith Street,
London W1V 5TZ, UK.

Music Sales Corporation,
225 Park Avenue South,
New York, NY 10003, USA.

Music Sales Pty Ltd.,
120 Rothschild Avenue,
Rosebery, NSW 2018, Australia.

To the Music Trade only:
Music Sales Limited,
8/9 Frith Street,
London W1V 5TZ, UK.

Originally published by Loeb Uitgevers BV, Amsterdam, Holland. All picture rights
cleared at source.

Typeset by Capital Setters, London W1.
Printed by Courier International Limited, Tiptree, Essex.

Every effort has been made to trace the copyright holders of the photographs in this
book but one or two were unreachable. We would be grateful if the photographers
concerned would contact us.

CONTENTS

introduction

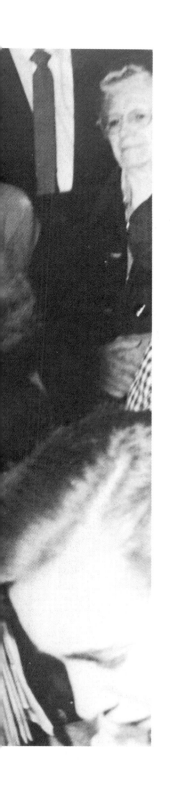

Marilyn Monroe was the greatest photographic model the world has ever known. Her medium was the photograph, and all her life revolved around photographs. She was discovered through photography, she became popular through photographs, her marriages came about through photographs, her divorces were caused by photographs. Marilyn Monroe is remembered not because of a handful of classic films but through thousands and thousands of wonderful photographs.

It was only after 17 B-movies and two powerful supporting roles that Marilyn was allowed to star in a film of real substance: *Gentlemen Prefer Blondes* by Howard Hawkes. This was in 1953 and by this time Marilyn was already a superstar thanks to her photographs. She was unquestionably a great actress who often overshadowed everything and everyone else in her films; in *Gentlemen Prefer Blondes*, *The Seven Year Itch* and *Some Like It Hot* she attracted all the attention on to herself. The third in this trio was also a gigantic hit at the box-office, but Marilyn's personal popularity far overshadowed the popularity of her films.

Eve Arnold, a top photographer associated with Monroe in the early 50s, writes in her book about Marilyn: "She knew that she was superior when she was being photographed, and she liked it a lot. She didn't need to learn scripts as she did in her films. She could let her imagination flow freely without bothering about contents and continuity, and for every photographer and every picture she could be a different Marilyn. It was always her party and often there was champagne and music, and she was always the centre of attention. She may have invented Marilyn herself, but she had many helpers – the photographers who photographed her.

John Springer, Marilyn's PR for many years, says: "You could speak to her about her last film which might have been a triumph. That was okay, she was pleased about that. But when you spoke to her about her last photo session… that was when her eyes really sparkled.

Marilyn, never a natural actress, actually became the greatest star the camera has ever seen. Thousands of pictures confirm this, and only Marilyn herself can add to this legacy. She did this in numerous interviews which together tell the story of her life.

There have been countless biographies of Marilyn Monroe but never an autobiography. This is the nearest thing to it.

Guus Luijters

youth

Marilyn Monroe's earliest memory is of the time that she was taken home,
still a baby, by her grandmother who later went insane.
'I remember waking up from my nap fighting for my life.
Something was pressed against my face. It could have been a
pillow. I fought with all my strength.'

'I don't remember seeing my father. I don't know what he looked
like, I've been told he was a tall, thin man, good-looking with a
moustache. I've never heard from him. I've been told he was killed
in an automobile accident when I was six months old. My father is
Abraham Lincoln – I mean I think of Lincoln as my father. He was
wise and kind and good. He is my ideal, Lincoln, I love him.'

'My birth certificate reads Norma Jean Mortenson. I was told that
my father was killed in an automobile accident before I was born,
so that is what I've always told people. There was no way I could
check on that. I was brought up as an orphan. I have had eleven or

twelve sets of foster parents. I don't want to count them all again, to see whether there were really eleven or twelve. I hope you won't ask me to. It depresses me. Some families kept me longer; others got tired of me in a short time. I must have made them nervous or something.'

Marilyn's mother worked in one of the film studios. She never knew her father but would often dream that he was Clark Gable, or some other famous movie star, who would one day come and whisk her away . . .
'The only thing I really remember is that I was all by myself. All alone. For so long. My mother's name was Gladys Monroe Baker, and my real name was Norma Jean Baker. They changed it when

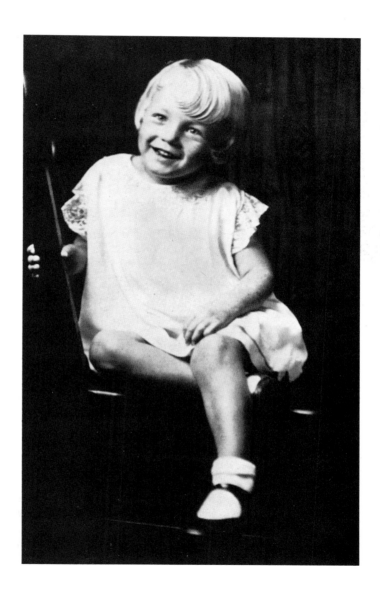

they decided to build me up. They change whatever they want to.

'I was a mistake. My mother didn't want to have me. I guess she never wanted me. I probably got in her way. I know I must have disgraced her. A divorced woman has enough problems in getting a man, I guess, but one with an illegitimate baby . . . I wish . . . I still wish . . . she had wanted me.

'I kept thinking when I was at these people's homes, these strange homes, I kept thinking, hoping that one day, a nice man

would come and say, "I'm here to take my daughter." Then I would have been safe. I kept hoping. Sometimes I remember even dressing up in whatever clothes I had, thinking that this was the day he'd come. I wanted to be ready. But he never came. No one ever came . . .'

'I was never used to being happy, so that wasn't something I ever took for granted. You see, I was brought up differently from the average American child because the average child is brought up expecting to be happy – that's it, successful, happy and on time.'

'As I grew older I knew I was different from other children because there were no kisses or promises in my life. I often felt lonely and wanted to die. I would try to cheer myself up with daydreams. I never dreamed of anyone loving me as I saw other children loved. That was too big a stretch for my imagination. I compromised by dreaming of my attracting someone's attention (besides God), of having people look at me and say my name.'

After a long series of foster homes, Marilyn was sent to an orphanage.
'At least before, I was with people. They may not have wanted me, but it was better than the Home. That was like prison. Besides, I wasn't really an orphan. An orphan doesn't have any parents. All the other kids there had parents that were dead. I had at least one parent. But she didn't want me. I was too ashamed to try to explain it to the other kids there . . .

'Dishes, dishes, dishes. I knew I was going to grow up to be a dishwasher. That's all I ever learned.

'I never felt like I belonged, even at the Home. The only time I was happy was when they took us to a movie. I loved movies. That was the only fun I ever had. The stars were my friends. That was my freedom.'

'The first family I lived with told me I couldn't go to the movies because it was sinful. I listened to them say the world was coming to an end, and if I was doing something sinful when it happened, I'd go down below, below, below. So the few times I was able to sneak into a movie, I spent most of the time there praying the world wouldn't end while I was inside.'

Marilyn's foster parents were not substitute families in the true sense.
They were simply paid to look after her for a certain period.
'Nobody ever called me their daughter. No one ever held me.
No one kissed me. Nobody. And I was afraid to call anyone
"Mom" or "Dad". I knew I didn't have any. They knew, too.
What could I say?

   'They had kids of their own, and when Christmas came there
was a big tree and all the kids in the house got presents but me.
One of the other kids gave me an orange. I can remember that
Christmas Day, eating that orange all by myself . . .'

'No one ever told me I was pretty when I was a little girl. All little
girls should be told they're pretty, even if they aren't.'

'I had one pair of foster parents and, when I was about ten, they
made me promise never to drink when I grew up, and I signed a
pledge never to smoke or swear. My next foster family gave me
empty whisky bottles for playthings. With them, and with empty
cigarette packages, I played store. I guess I must have had the
finest collection of empty whisky bottles and empty cigarette
packages any girl ever had. I'd line them up on a plank beside the
road, and when people drove along I'd say, "Wouldn't you like
some whisky?"

   'I remember some of the people in the cars driving past my
"whisky" store saying, "Imagine! Why, it's *terrible*."

   'Looking back, I guess I used to play-act all the time. For one
thing, it meant I could live in a more interesting world than the
one around me.'

'When I was eleven years old the door to the real world suddenly
opened for me. Even the girls paid attention to me, because they
thought: "Hmm, this is someone to reckon with!" I had to walk to
school, two miles there and two miles back. All the men whistled
– you know, labourers on their way to work. The world started to
like me. Newspaper-boys delivered their newspaper personally to
our house. I often hung from the branch of the tree just for fun
while I was wearing an old tight sweater. I did not realise what
kind of effect such a sweater had. So the newspaper-boys used to
drop by, on their bicycles and give me a free newspaper, which the
family where I lived appreciated.

'I found it a bit frightening to come down. I let myself be
lowered onto the pavement and then I kicked a bit against the
pavement and against the leaves and then I'd say something, but
usually I just listened. And then sometimes my foster parents
would start to worry because I'd laugh so loudly and happily.
I think they thought it was hysteria. But it was just that sudden
freedom. If I asked the boys, "Can I borrow your bike" they'd
always say, "Of course," and then I'd just ride off, laughing in the
wind. And the boys would just stand there waiting for me to come
back. But I loved the wind. The wind freed me . . .'

'While I was in the fifth grade, the school picked me out to appear
in the Easter Eve service at the Hollywood Bowl. They gave all
of us a black domino. Under that, we were wearing white tunics.
The service, which is really impressive, begins before sunrise,
with all the children set out in the shape of a cross. Just at the
moment when the sun was rising, we were given the signal to take
off the black dominoes, which changed the black cross into a white

cross. But I was so interested in gazing up at the sky that I didn't
pay attention and didn't see the signal. I was the only child who
forgot to remove her black robe. I was the only black spot on a
white cross.'

'This need to attract attention played a part, I think, in the problems I had on Sundays at church. No sooner had I sat down on my bench with the organ playing and the congregation singing hymns all together, than I'd feel an irresistible urge to take off all my clothes. I desperately wanted to stand up, completely naked, so that God and the others would look at me. I had to clench my teeth and sit on my hands to stop myself from undressing. Sometimes, it got so bad that I had to pray hard and beg the Lord to give me the strength to stay dressed.'

'My impulse to appear naked and my dreams about it had no shame or sense of sin in them. Dreaming of people looking at me made me feel less lonely. I think I wanted them to see me naked because I was ashamed of the clothes I wore – the never-changing faded blue dress of poverty. Naked, I was like the other girls and not someone in an orphan's uniform.'

'I dreamed of myself walking proudly in beautiful clothes and being admired by everyone and overhearing words of praise. I made up the praises and repeated them aloud as if someone else were saying them.'

'When I was a kid, some of my foster parents would send me to the movies so I wouldn't hang around, getting in their way. I'd stay there the whole day and part of the evening, in the first row, a little girl all alone in front of the giant screen, and I adored it. I loved everything, everything that moved up front, I didn't miss a thing – and I didn't need popcorn.'

'People are eager to see me. And I remember the years I was unwanted. All the hundreds of times nobody wanted to see the little servant girl, Norma Jean, not even her mother. I feel a queer satisfaction in punishing the people who are wanting me now. But it's not them I'm really punishing. It's the long-ago people who didn't want Norma Jean . . . the later I am, the happier Norma Jean grows.'

Marilyn Monroe stuttered as a child:
'Even now, the stuttering comes back sometimes, when I'm too nervous or over-excited. Once, I had a small part with a scene in

which I had to climb a staircase. I've forgotten what happened, but the assistant director rushed over to me, shouting, and I was so upset that, during the retake, I couldn't bring out my line! Only some awful mumbling. Whereupon the director, furious, also rushed over and shouted: "You don't actually stutter?" "Y-y-you th-th-think not?" I said to him . . .'

'It isn't Marilyn Monroe in the tub, but Norma Jean. I'm giving

Norma Jean a treat. She used to have to bathe in water used by six or eight other people. Now she can bathe in water as clean and transparent as a pane of glass. And it seems that Norma Jean can't get enough of fresh bath water that smells of real perfume.'

Marilyn's life was sometimes described as 'the perfect Cinderella story . . .'
'I don't know where they got that: I haven't ended with a prince. I've never had even one fairy godmother. Maybe they're thinking of a rags-to-riches routine. Not that I'm rich yet, but things are beginning to work out.'

model

Marilyn first became a popular model in 1942 . . .

'That company not only made planes, it made parachutes. For a
while I inspected parachutes. Then they quit letting us girls do
that. They had the parachutes inspected on the outside, but I don't
think it was because of my inspecting. Then I was in the dope
room spraying dope on fuselages. Dope is liquid stuff, like banana
oil and glue mixed.

'I was out on sick leave for a few days, and when I came back
the Army photographers from the Hal Roach Studios, where they
had the Army photographic headquarters, were around taking
photographs and snapping and shooting while I was doping those
ships. The Army guys saw me and asked, "Where had *you* been?"

' "I've been on sick leave," I said.

' "Come outside," they told me. "We're going to take your
picture."

' "I can't," I said. "The other ladies here in the dope room will
give me trouble if I stop doing what I'm doing and go out with
you." That didn't discourage those Army photographers. They
got special permission for me to go outside from Mr Whosis, the
president of the plant. For a while they posed me rolling ships;
then they asked me, "Don't you have a sweater?"

' "Yes," I told them, "it so happens that I brought one with me.
It's in my locker." After that I rolled ships around in a sweater.
A photographer kept telling me, "You should be a model," but I
thought he was flirting. Several weeks later, he brought the colour
shots he'd taken of me, and he said the Eastman Kodak Company
had asked him, "Who's your model, for goodness' sake?"

'So I began to think that maybe he wasn't kidding about how
I ought to be a model. Then I found that a girl could make five
dollars an hour modelling, which was different from working ten
hours a day for the kind of money I'd been making at the plane
plant. And it was a long way from the orphanage, where I'd been
paid five cents a week for working in the dining room or ten cents
a month for working in the pantry. And out of those big sums, a
penny every Sunday had to go into the church collection. I never
could figure why they took a penny from an orphan for that.'

'There was still a lot of sex. The guys sort of expected it as part of
the job. But now instead of paying me, they'd take my picture.

And I liked that better. I loved to pose. I was amazed how the
pictures usually made me look better than I was in real life.'

'I wore a certain red dress to a party at the Beverly Hills Hotel. It
was a beautiful dress. It cost a fortune. I got it at I. Magnin's. It
was a copy of a French original. But one lady columnist wrote that
I was cheap and vulgar in it and that I would have looked better in
a potato sack. So, somebody in studio publicity asked, "So, O.K.,
why don't we shoot old Marilyn in a potato sack?"

'That was fine with me, as long as they let me wear long,
dangling earrings and a bracelet four inches wide. I don't know
about the more than four hundred newspapers, but I do know
that shot was printed all over the country. As a result, a potato
company in Twin Falls, Idaho, sent me a sack of potatoes. There

was a potato shortage on then, and the boys in the publicity stole
them all. I never saw one. It just goes to show why I always ask,
"Can you trust a publicity man or can't you?" '

'When the studio first heard about the calendar, everybody there
was in a frenzy. They telephoned me on the set where I was
working in a quickie called _Don't Bother to Knock_. The person who
called asked me, "What's all this about a calendar of you in the
nude? Did you do it?"

‘ "Yes," I said. "Is there anything wrong with that? So they've
found out it's me on that calendar! Well, what do you know!"
‘ "Found out!" he almost screamed. "There you are, all of you,

in full colour!'' Then he must have gotten mixed up, for first he
said, "Just deny everything." Then he said, "Don't say anything.
I'll be right down."

'I was working on the Fox Western Avenue lot when this
worried man came tearing in wringing his hands. He took me into
my dressing room to talk about the dreadful thing I'd done in
posing for such a photograph. I could think of nothing else to say,
so I said apologetically, "I thought the lighting the photographer

used would disguise me." I thought that man would have a stroke
when I said that.'

"There was still a lot of sex. The guys sort of
expected it as part of the job. But now instead
of paying me, they'd take my picture."

'What had happened was that I was behind in my rent at the
Hollywood Studio Club, where girls live who hope to crash the
movies. You're only supposed to get one week behind in your rent
at the club, but they must have felt sorry for me because they'd

given me three warnings. A lot of photographers had asked me to pose in the nude, but I'd always said "No." I was getting five dollars an hour for plain modelling, but the price for nude modelling was fifty an hour. So I called Tom Kelley, a photographer I knew, and said, "They're kicking me out of here. How soon can we do it?" He said, "We can do it tomorrow."

'I didn't even have to get dressed, so it didn't take long. I mean it takes longer to get dressed than it does to get undressed. I'd asked Tom, "Please don't have anyone else there except your wife, Natalie." He said, "O.K." He only made two poses. There was a shot of me sitting up and a shot of me lying down. I think the one of me lying down is the best.

'Just before I went back to Fox to work in *Don't Bother to Knock*, I'd been at RKO on a loan-out, working in a picture called *Clash by Night*. While I was at RKO, mysterious people kept calling up Jerry Wald, who was in charge of production there, and trying to blackmail him by saying they were going to break a story about me having posed in the nude for a calendar, and that news like that

would put the kiss of death on *Clash by Night* if Mr Wald didn't do
thus and so for them.

'I'm saving a copy of it for my grandchildren. There's a place in
Los Angeles which even reproduces it on bras or panties. But I
have only autographed a few copies of it, mostly for sick people.
And I signed one for the cameraman on the picture in which I was
working when the calendar story broke. On one I wrote, "This
may not be my best angle," and on another I wrote, "Do you like
me better with long hair?" '

*In reply to the question of whether she'd want to be photographed as
'the girl-next-door':*
'The whole thing is too ridiculous, I'd let any magazine in to
photograph the little I do around the house. They wouldn't be
interested but I can assure you that I am not baking cakes.'

'First I was shown an album with the most beautiful pictures I'd
ever seen of people he had photographed. I said: "They're so
beautiful! Who took them?" There was a young man standing
there the whole time. I said: "I want him to photograph me."
I said I had a heavy schedule but that I'd pose all night. I said:
"Where is he?" It was the young man standing there. I said: "He's
a kid." He's thirty-two, but I think he looks like nineteen. I'd like
him to always photograph me. I've been photographed a lot, but
with Milton Greene I discovered a new aspect, new hope. I never
really liked the way I was photographed until I saw Milton's
pictures. Milton has a gift . . . he's not only a photographer, he's
really an artist. Even with fashion, which is usually boring, he can
do something so beautiful! I work with other good photographers,
but he's a great artist. He's very original . . . people are going to

With Milton Greene

talk about him a lot. He's a very . . . one of the things that makes him such an artist is his sensitivity, his sense of introspection. It was the first time I didn't have to pose. He gave me time to think, but his camera was constantly working away. I didn't even know it. I met Milton two days before he got married. When I heard about it, I was very sad, but only for about five minutes.'

starlet

During the time that Marilyn Monroe was still married to Jim Dougherty and he was at sea, she hung around in cafés, among other places, to kill the time.

'These bars were full of agents. Or at least guys who claimed they were. A lot of the girls who hung out there hoped they would break into movies that way. This agent really liked me, I think. We met a few times. He told me that I was special, and that I had the looks to be in movies. He said that if I did *this*, what I was doing, with the right men, I might be able to be in pictures. I laughed at him and told him I couldn't act. And he said neither can so-and-so or so-and-so. He named some of the big actresses then. I thought about it after he left. You know, I decided, maybe he was right. At first, it was just a thought. But it got bigger and bigger. It became my ambition, my only ambition, the first one I ever had.'

'Everybody in Hollywood was there to check over the new girls. We had our choice. We could be picked up by some handsome young actor and have a little fun. Or we could go off with some old bigwig and make a few dollars, or, if we were really lucky, we

could get him to help us find a part. Most of us always tried to find
an old guy. I got to be known pretty quick. They considered me a
"hot number" back then.'

About her first screen test:
'Blonde hair and breasts, that's how I got started. I couldn't act.
All I had was my blonde hair and a body men liked. The reason
I got ahead is that I was lucky and met the right men.'

'I had appeared on five magazine covers. Mostly men's magazines,
with cover girls who aren't flat-chested. I was on *See* four or five
months in a row. Each time they changed my name. One month
I was Norma Jean Dougherty – they used my first husband's
name. The second month I was Jean Norman. I don't know
what other names they used, but I must have looked different
each time.'

**"Most of us always tried to find an old guy. I got
to be known pretty quick. They considered me a
'hot number' back then."**

'There were different poses – outdoors, indoors, but mostly just
sitting looking over the Pacific. That brought in the swimsuit idea.
You looked at those pictures and you didn't see much ocean, but
you saw a lot of me.
    'One of the magazines I was on wasn't a man's magazine at all.
It was called *Family Circle.* You buy it in supermarkets. I was
holding a lamb with a pinafore. I was the one with the pinafore.
But on most covers I had on things like a striped towel. The towel
was striped because the cover was to be in colour and the stripes
were the colour, and there was a big fan blowing on the towel and
on my hair. That was right after my first divorce, and I needed to
earn a living bad. I couldn't type. I didn't know how to do
anything. So Howard Hughes had an accident.
    'He was in hospital and Hedda Hopper wrote in her column:
"Howard Hughes must be recuperating because he sent out for
photographs of a new girl he's seen on five different magazines."
Right after that, Howard Hughes's casting director got my
telephone number, and he got in touch with me, and he said
Howard Hughes wanted to see me.

'But he must have forgotten or changed his mind or something, because instead of going to see him, I went over to the Fox Studio with a fellow named Harry Lipton, who handled my photographic modelling.

'Expensive cars used to drive up beside me when I was standing on a street corner or walking on a sidewalk, and the driver would say, "I could do something for you in pictures. How would you like to be a Goldwyn girl?"

'I figured those guys in those cars were trying for a pickup, and I had an agent so I could say to those fellows, "See my agent."

That's how I happened to be handled by Harry Lipton.

    'When Ben Lyon saw me, he said, "You're the first girl I've discovered since Jean Harlow who I'm sure will make it." '

"Howard Hughes must be recuperating because he sent out for photographs of a new girl he's seen on five different magazines."

Once Marilyn Monroe had been signed to a contract with Fox, no-one was satisfied with her name, which at that time was Norma Jean Baker, or Mortensen, or Dougherty.

With Ben Lyon

'Ben Lyon of Fox has changed my name. I reminded him of two women: Jean Harlow and a girl called Marilyn Miller. When they started considering a new name for me I asked if I could keep my mother's maiden name: Monroe. So the question was whether I should be called Jean Monroe or Marilyn Monroe. That same

evening some kids asked me for an autograph and I did not know how to spell Marilyn and I had to ask someone.'

Marilyn posed for endless publicity pictures, including one series to accompany the story that she had been a baby-sitter discovered by a Fox talent scout.
'They could at least have had me be a daddy-sitter.'

Marilyn Monroe was in Atlantic City to pose with all the candidates
for the Miss America title. There she was approached by someone
from the army who had the idea of getting her to pose with the
'real Miss Americas', a Wac, a Wave and a Waf.
   'And then that man got the idea to stand on a chair to take the
photograph so that the camera could look a long way inside my dress.'
   The photo didn't attract much attention and all the newspapers threw
it out until a top army official banned publication of the photograph on the
grounds that it showed too much of Marilyn. Instantly, the photo became
national news and despite the fact that it was late, Marilyn Monroe got
out of bed to answer the phone and comment:

'I am very surprised and very hurt. I wasn't aware that my neckline was too low. I'd noticed people looking at me all day, but I thought they were admiring my Grand Marshal's badge.'

"That evening some kids asked me for an autograph and I did not know how to spell Marilyn and I had to ask someone."

Marilyn tried hard to persuade Darryl Zanuck to let her play more demanding roles . . .

'His idea was that no one would pay their money for a ticket to see me in a decent role. I would have been happy to do anything – you know – to get him to let me try something different. He wasn't interested at all. Every other guy was. Why wasn't he?'

With Rand Brooks in Ladies Of The Chorus

With John Huston on the set of
The Asphalt Jungle

Marilyn Monroe was sent on a publicity tour for Love Happy. *She knew that she would be going to New York and Chicago and, because of the temperatures she expected there, bought only woollen clothes with her expense money. When she arrived in New York, though, it was during a heat wave.*

'Mr Gowan's agent, who was in charge of my publicity tour, could cope with anything. "You have to make the most of what you have," he explained. He had the idea of making me pose on the carriage steps, my face running with sweat, holding an ice-cream cone in each hand. The caption on the photo said: "Marilyn Monroe, the screen's hottest blonde, cooling herself." '

'When I started out in movies, I used to go to night school. The headmistress didn't know who I was and couldn't understand why boys from other classes sometimes popped their heads through the door during a class to look at me and whisper. One day, she decided to ask my classmates, who told her I acted in movies. She said: "And I took her for a young girl straight out of a convent!" That's one of the biggest compliments I've ever been paid.'

In There's No Business Like
Show Business

"Expensive cars used to drive up beside me
when I was standing on a street corner or
walking on a sidewalk, and the driver would
say, 'I could do something for you in the
pictures. How would you like to be a
Goldwyn girl?' "

star

'It is the public that made me a star – if I am a star – the public, not the studio, not one particular person . . . the public.'

'The time when I sort of began to think I was famous I was driving somebody to the airport and as I came back there was this movie house and I saw my name in lights. I pulled the car up at a distance down the street – it was too much to take up close, you know – all of a sudden. And I said, 'God, somebody's made a mistake.' But there it was, in lights. And I sat there and said, 'So that's the way it looks,' and yet at the studio they had said, 'Remember you're not a star.' Yet there it is up in lights.'

'I really got the idea I must be a star, or *something*, from the newspapermen – I'm saying men, not the women – who would interview me and they would be warm and friendly. By the way, that part of the press, you know, the men of the press, unless they have their own personal quirks against me, they were always very warm and friendly and they'd say, 'You know, you're the only star,' and I'd say, 'Star?' and they'd look at me as if I were nuts. I think they, in their own kind of way, made me realize I was famous.'

'I kept driving past the theater with my name on the marquee. 'Marilyn Monroe'. Was I excited. I wished they were using Norma Jean so that all the kids at the Home and schools who never noticed me could see it.'

When Marilyn obtained her first major film contract she was heard to say: 'Well, that's the last cock *I* have to suck.'

In 1953, Marilyn Monroe received the Photoplay Prize for most popular actress of the year. At the awards ceremony and accompanying dinner, she wore a rather daring dress, which elicited the following comment from Joan Crawford: 'Sex plays a tremendously important part in every person's life. People are interested in it, intrigued by it. But they don't like to see it flaunted in their faces . . . They should tell Miss Monroe that the public likes provocative feminine personalities, but it also likes to know that underneath it all, the actresses are ladies.'
'I think the thing that hit me hardest about Miss Crawford's story

is that it came from her. I've always admired her for being such a wonderful mother – for taking four children and giving them a fine home. Who, better than I, knows what it means to homeless little ones?'

"I liked the fact that the movie salesmen who came to Hollywood for a big studio sales rally whistled loudest and longest when I entered their midst."

When Marilyn Monroe received a prize from the Italian film industry, Anna Magnani was also present at the awards ceremony. As she left, Magnani shouted 'Putani!' ('Whore') . . .
'These women movie stars never get along with me. They hate me on sight, so I've given up trying to make them like me.'

With Anna Magnani

'I remember when I got the part in *Gentlemen Prefer Blondes*, Jane Russell – she was the brunette in it and I was the blonde – she got $200,000 for it and I got my $500 a week, but that to me was, you know, considerable. She, by the way, was quite wonderful to me. The only thing was I couldn't get a dressing room. I said, finally –

I really got to this kind of level – I said, 'Look, after all, I *am* the blonde and it is *Gentlemen Prefer Blondes!*' Because still they kept saying, 'Remember, you're not a star'. I said, 'Well, whatever I am, I *am* the blonde!' '

In Gentlemen Prefer Blondes

'Everybody in the studio wanted me as a star in his movie. I finally went into *Gentlemen Prefer Blondes*, and after that, *How to Marry a Millionaire*. I liked doing these pictures. I liked the fact that I was important in making them a great financial success and that my studio cleaned up a fortune, despite the fact that its chiefs had considered me unphotogenic. I liked the fact that the movie salesmen who came to Hollywood for a big studio sales rally whistled loudest and longest when I entered their midst.'

'When Jane Russell and I were together in the cast of *Gentlemen Prefer Blondes*, we were asked to put our footprints in wet concrete in front of Grauman's Chinese Theater, along with the dent left by Jimmy Durante's nose and the print of one of Betty Grable's legs. I suggested that Jane lean over the wet cement and that I sit down in it and we could leave our prints that way, but my idea was vetoed. After that I suggested that Grauman's use a diamond to dot the 'I' in the Marilyn I scratched in the wet concrete. They finally compromised on dotting it with a rhinestone, but some sightseer chiselled that rhinestone out.'

'If I'd observed all the rules, I'd never have got anywhere.'

'I used to say to myself, 'What the devil have you got to be
proud about, Marilyn Monroe?' And I'd answer, 'Everything,

everything,' and I'd walk slowly and turn my head slowly as if I were a queen.'

'The only trouble with becoming famous as a result of a half-dozen scandalous happenings is that the scandal-made star can't just rest on her old scandals. If she wants to keep her high place in the public eye and on the Hollywood producers' casting list she

has to keep getting into more and more hot water. After you're thirty-five, getting into romantic hot water is a little difficult, and getting yourself publicized in love triangles and café duels over your favours needs not only smart press agents but also a little miracle to help out.'

'Success came to me in a rush. It surprised my employers much more than it did me. Even when I had played only bit parts in a few films, all the movie magazines and newspapers started printing my picture and giving me write-ups. I used to tell lies in my interviews – chiefly about my mother and father. I'd say she was dead and he was somewhere in Europe. I lied because I was ashamed to have the world know my mother was in a mental institution – and that I had been born 'out of wedlock' and never heard my illegal father's voice.'

'I couldn't believe it. There were thousands of them screaming for me. I was scared, but I'd do it again. I never believed all the fan mail I got was real until I sang for the troops in Korea. Wow! They really liked me.'

'When I travel it's always the same. No matter where I go or why I go there, it all ends up the same way. I've never seen anything. Becoming a movie star is like living on a merry-go-round.'

'I feel as though it's all happening to someone right next to me. I'm close, I can feel it, I can hear it, but it isn't really me.'

'I flew into New York at eight o'clock one morning and there were all those photographers waiting to take pictures of me at the airport, and all that morning I had a series of interviews with newspaper people. Those interviews came twenty minutes or a half hour apart. Then I was rushed to a luncheon with a group of magazine people, and right after luncheon I tore over to the Daily

News Building. I don't think anybody can take that kind of a routine very long.

'Another complication is that I have a certain sort of stupid sincerity. I mean I don't want to tell everybody who interviews me the same thing. I want them all to have something new and different and exclusive. When I worry about that, I start to get sick at my stomach.'

'I refuse to let articles appear in movie magazines signed "By Marilyn Monroe". I might never see that article and it might be okayed by somebody in the studio. This is wrong, because when

I was a little girl I read signed stories in fan magazines and
I believed every word the stars said in them. Then I'd try to model
my life after the lives of the stars I read about. If I'm going to have
that kind of influence, I want to be sure it's because of something
I've actually said or written.'

'It stirs up envy, fame does. People you run into feel that, well,
who is she – who does she think she is, Marilyn Monroe? They
feel fame gives them some kind of privilege to walk up to you and
say anything to you, you know, of any kind of nature – and it
won't hurt your feelings – like it's happening to your clothing.'

'Early in the morning, when I take a look outside, garbage collectors on 57th Street say: "Hi, Marilyn! How are you this morning?" It's an honour for me, and I love them for it. Those workers! All I have to do is walk past them and they whistle.'

Sometimes Marilyn would go out with no make-up, wearing dark glasses and a headscarf . . .
'In spite of that, I've had people stop me and say, "I know who you are." And I tell them, "Oh, no, you're wrong. I'm Sheree North," or "I'm Mamie Van Doren."
    ' "Oh no you're not!" they tell me. "We recognise the voice." '

'I knew I belonged to the audience, that I belonged to the world, not because of my talent, not even because I was beautiful, but because I never belonged to any one individual. The public was my only family, my only Prince Charming, the only house I had ever dreamed of.'

'I don't care about the critics. I don't care about anybody. The

only people I care about are the people in Times Square, across the street from the theater, who can't get close as I come in. If I had light make-up on, they'd never see me. This make-up is for them, so that when I wave to them it will soften out in the distance across the square.'

During a parade in Atlantic City

'. . . It has gotten me into trouble. Telling the truth, I mean. When I get into trouble being too direct and I try to pull back, people think I'm coy.

'My reputation for being "direct" is not good for me. You take what I'm supposed to have said about disliking being interviewed by women reporters, but that with gentlemen of the press it's different, because we have a mutual appreciation of being male and

female. Well I didn't say that I disliked women reporters. As dumb
as I am, I wouldn't be that dumb, although that in itself is kind
of a mysterious remark because people don't really know how
dumb I am. But I honestly prefer men reporters. They're more
stimulating. That's probably why.'

*Following the baby which she said she had as a teenager, and several
miscarriages, Marilyn Monroe underwent an operation in the hope that
she would be able to have children again . . .*
'What good is it being Marilyn Monroe? Why can't I just be an
ordinary woman? A woman who can have a family. A family? I'd
settle for just one baby. My own baby. Oh, why do things have to
work out so rotten?

'I'm so stupid. It's my fault. I had already given up on babies.
But then there was this operation. It seemed like a ray of hope.
So I got all excited again. I shouldn't have . . .

'If I can't be a mother, I better be an actress. I have to be
something. And, whatever it is, I'm gonna be good at it!'

'The fact that I'm famous gives me a feeling of happiness but it's
only temporary. It's like caviar: caviar is nice, but to have caviar
every day at every meal . . . I live for my work and for the few
people I can count on, but one day my fame will be over and
I will say "goodbye fame; I have had you, and I always knew you
wouldn't last. It's been an interesting experience but not my
whole life." '

When she was fired from her part in Something's Got to Give, *she was terrified that she would disappear completely from the public eye:* 'If I were in *Playboy*, that would sure make everyone know I'm still around.'

acting

Marilyn was always eager to be in the public eye.
'It's better for the whole world to know you, even as a sex star, than never to be known at all. If I'm that famous, I'll get the

good parts soon enough. I'm not going to kill myself by trying to rush it.'

'Acting was something golden and beautiful. It wasn't an art. It was like a game you played that enabled you to step out of the dull world you knew into worlds so bright they made your heart leap just to think of them.'

'When I was younger, I used to go to Grauman's Chinese Theater and try to fit my foot in the prints in the cement there. And I'd say, "Oh, oh, my foot's too big, I guess that's out." I did have a funny feeling later when I finally put my foot down into that wet cement. I sure knew what it really meant to me – anything's possible, almost.'

'Acting isn't something you do. Instead of doing it, it occurs . . .
if you're going to start with logic, you might as well give up.
You can have conscious preparation, but you must have
unconscious results.'

*Joe DiMaggio wanted Marilyn to forget about acting altogether. He loved
her for herself, and wanted her to be his wife – full time. He was a rich
man and she didn't need a career to support herself. But despite Joe's
attitude, Marilyn was as determined as ever . . .*
'He didn't believe that I had any talent to fall back on. That scared
me to death. I wanted a career, and even though I couldn't act
then, I sure wanted to learn. He thought I was the best woman
there was, but he never believed I could act. Besides, Joe said that
even if I could act like Bette Davis, the studios still wouldn't give
me the parts I wanted. "You're trapped as a dumb blonde. That's
it," he said. Well, I wanted to prove myself – to him and to me.
    'I had always been nothing, a nobody. Then I had a chance to be

With Tommy Rettig in River
Of No Return

somebody. I couldn't give it up, just when things were looking
good for me. Not just to be a housewife, even Joe's housewife. I
had to see if I could be a success on my own . . . That was then.
Now when I talk to Joe and tell him what I'm going through, he
just says, "I told you," and I keep thinking that he wasn't wrong.
But, honest, I love being a star. After all I've been through,
I won't quit now.'

'You don't have to know anything to dream hard. I knew nothing
about acting. I had never read a book about it, or tried to do it,
or discussed it with anyone. I was ashamed to tell the few people

*Just before her divorce at the
premiere of* The Seven Year
Itch

I knew of what I was dreaming.'

'Studio bosses are jealous of their power. They are like political bosses. They want to pick out their own candidate for public office. They don't want the public rising up and dumping a girl . . . in their laps and saying, "Make her a star." '

"I knew how third-rate I was. I could actually feel my lack of talent, as if it were cheap clothes I was wearing inside. But, my God, how I wanted to learn."

With Tom Ewell in The Seven Year Itch

'There were dozens of us on the set, bit players, with a gesture to make and a line or two to recite. Some of them were veteran bit players. After ten years in the movies they were still saying one line and walking ten feet towards nowhere. A few were young and had nice bosoms but I knew they were different from me. They didn't have my illusions. My illusions didn't have anything to do with being a fine actress. I knew how third-rate I was. I could

actually feel my lack of talent, as if it were cheap clothes I was
wearing inside. But, my God, how I wanted to learn, to change,
to improve! I didn't want anything else. Not men, not money,
not love, but the ability to act. With the arc lights on me and the
camera pointed at me, I suddenly knew myself. How clumsy,
empty, uncultured I was! A sullen orphan with a goose egg
for a head.'

*With Buddy Adler, producer at
20th Century Fox*

'In Hollywood a girl's virtue is much less important than her
hair-do. You're judged by how you look, not by what you are.
Hollywood's a place where they'll pay you a thousand dollars for a
kiss, and fifty cents for your soul. I know, because I turned down
the first offer often enough and held out for the fifty cents.'

With Cary Grant and Charles
Coburn in Monkey Business

After the première of How to Marry a Millionaire:
'I guess this is just about the happiest night of my life. Somehow
it's like when I was a little girl and pretended wonderful things
were happening to me. Now they are . . .

   'It's funny how success makes so many people hate you. I wish
it wasn't that way. It would be wonderful to enjoy success without
seeing envy in the eyes of those around you.'

'In Hollywood, millions and billions of dollars have been earned,
but there is no monument or museum in sight. I do not consider
your footprint at the front of Grauman's Chinese theater a
monument, although at the time it meant a lot to me. Nobody
leaves anything in Hollywood. I am talking here about the people
who made millions, not the ordinary labourers.'

'I think I have one talent, I think it's observing. I hope that it adds
up to acting. I hope to put it to good use.'

'I don't feel as hopeless as I did. I don't know why it is. I've read
a little of Freud and it might have to do with what he said. I think

he was on the right track.

'I want to be a real actress instead of a superficial actress. Now for the first time I'm learning to use myself fully as an actress. I want to add something to what I had before. Some people thought that they were getting their money's worth when they saw me in *The Seven Year Itch*, but I want people to get even more for their money when they see me in the future. Only today a taxi driver said to me, "Why did they ever put you in that little stinker, *River of No Return*?"

'It was a good question . . . I'm with that taxi driver. He's my boy. Knowing what I know now, I wouldn't accept *River of No Return* today. I think that I deserve a better deal than a Z cowboy movie, in which the acting finishes second to the scenery and the CinemaScope process. The studio was CinemaScope-conscious

Signing her contract for Some Like It Hot *with producer Walter Mirisch*

then. That means that it was pushing the scenery instead of pushing actors and actressses.'

'I disappeared because if people won't listen to you, there's no point in talking to people. If they won't listen, you're just banging your head against a wall. If you can't do what they want to do, the thing is to leave. I never got a chance to learn anything in Hollywood. They worked me too fast. They rushed me from one picture into another.

   'And I know who started all those stories which were sent out about me after I left Hollywood the last time. A big studio has much power with certain columnists and with trade papers. One paper had an editorial about me that went something like this: "Marilyn Monroe is a very stupid girl to give up all the wonderful

In How To Marry A Millionaire

things the movie industry has done for her and go back to New York, hoping to learn to act!"

   'Those weren't the exact words of that editorial, but that was the idea. Well, if it was supposed to scare me, it didn't. When I read it and I realised that it wasn't frightening me, I felt strong. That's why I know.'

'It makes something in me happy to be late. People are waiting for

me. People are eager to see me. I remember all the years I was
unwanted, all the hundreds of times nobody wanted to see the
little servant girl, Norma Jean – not even her mother. And I feel a
queer sensation in punishing the people who are wanting me now.
But it's not them I'm really punishing. It's the long-ago people
who didn't want Norma Jean. The later I am, the happier she
grows. To me, it's remarkable that I get there at all.'

**"Everyone's just laughing at me. I hate it. Big
breasts, big ass, big deal. Can't I be anything
else? Gee, how long can you be sexy?"**

*Marilyn's first and foremost concern was to become a serious actress, and
she seemed both confused and resentful that Hollywood had built her up
into a great sex symbol.*
'I want to act. I really do. I had enough of all that Hollywood shit.
I guess I looked pretty good, but there were so many girls out
there who looked better. You should see it. It's like a beauty
contest. I guess I was lucky . . . For a while.
   'They tell you to cry one tear, and if you feel two and therefore
cry two, it's no good. If you change "the" to "a" in your lines,
they correct you. An actress is not a machine, but they treat you

*With Lauren Bacall and
Humphrey Bogart at the
premiere of* How To Marry
A Millionaire

With Robert Mitchum in River Of No Return

like one. A money machine.

'I did what they said, and all it got me was a lot of abuse. Everyone's just laughing at me. I hate it. Big breasts, big ass, big deal. Can't I be anything else? Gee, how long can you be sexy?'

On January 7, 1955, Marilyn Monroe and Milton Greene formed her film company, Marilyn Monroe Inc. It was clear that she wanted to play other kinds of roles in other kinds of films. One of the films often named was The Brothers Karamazov.

'I want to do dramatic parts, like *The Brothers Karamazov*. But I don't want to play the brothers. I want to play Grushenka. She's a girl. It's no temptation to me to do the same thing over and over. I want to keep growing as a person and as an actress . . . in Hollywood they never ask me my opinion. They just tell me what time to come to work . . . One of the things about leaving Hollywood and coming to New York and attending the Actors' Studio is that I feel I can afford to be more myself. After all, if I can't be myself, who can I be I would like to know.'

When Marilyn Monroe was studying at the Actors' Studio, a great deal of

speculation occurred as to whether a new Marilyn Monroe would appear.
Marilyn Monroe herself wanted something to change in any event.
'It will be up to the public but I have to satisfy something inside of
me, too. That doesn't mean that all of a sudden I'm going to play
old-maid parts. No matter how much a person learns about being
a better actress, a person isn't suddenly going to change and wear

In Bus Stop

high-necked, long-sleeved dresses and dye her hair black . . .
I was inspired to study acting by seeing my own pictures!

'Recently someone asked me, "What do you really want to do
here in New York. What do you want to be?" and I said to him,
"I want to be an artist." And then he asked, "Do you mean that
you want to paint?" It never occurred to him that I meant I wanted
to become an artist in the theatre.'

"No matter how much a person learns about
being a better actress, a person isn't suddenly
going to change and wear high-necked, long-
sleeved dresses and dye her hair black . . ."

Marilyn Monroe was well known for always arriving on the set too late for her takes.

'I guess people think that why I'm late is some kind of arrogance, and I think it is the opposite of arrogance . . . I do want to be prepared when I get there to give a good performance or whatever to the best of my ability.'

'I don't think I'm as late as I used to be, and once I arrived at a cocktail party on time and nobody was there. So what are you supposed to do – sit around? Of course it's a good way to get acquainted with the hostess – but usually the hostess isn't ready either.'

'During the shooting of *Some Like It Hot*, Billy Wilder would sometimes say after a shot was in the can: "Certain actors do and re-do the same scene, but they lose their spontaneity." But when

In Some Like It Hot

I do it over again, I feel that I'm relaxing a little more, and that perhaps I'll dare go a bit further at the next try. I'm shy, and when you're shy you can't help it. I'll probably never be daring and I don't know if I'll ever become a great actress . . . I have to find out how I work best, the way to make the most of my acting, whether it's good, bad, or indifferent.'

'A lot of people can be there on time and do nothing, which I have
seen them do, and you know, all sit around and sort of chit-
chatting and talking trivia about their social life. Gable said about
me, 'When she's there, she's there. All of her is there! She's there
to work.'

'You've read there was some actor that once said about me that
kissing me was like kissing Hitler. Well, I think that's *his* problem.
If I have to do intimate love scenes with somebody who really has
these kind of feelings toward me, then my fantasy can come into
play. In other words, out with him, in with my fantasy. He was
never there. He only said that because I wore prettier dresses than
he did.'

'How do you fight anxiety? First of all, by concentrating on
something else. At the Method, it's called "putting in order" . . .
Instead of thinking of what you're feeling when you meet

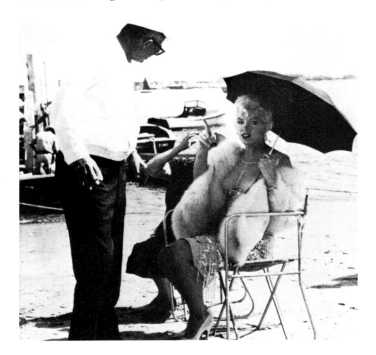

With Billy Wilder on the set of
Some Like It Hot

someone, just notice the strange or interesting things about him.
All you have to do is to direct your interest onto something other

than yourself. They say nervousness shows sensitivity. I don't get
great results myself, but enough, I think, to alter my relationship
with others. When you act, it's the same thing. Instead of thinking
"I'm an old ham", I start asking myself, "Why is Gable looking at
me that way? He must have his reasons." And so on.'

*Marilyn deeply resented the dumb blonde image which had been willed
upon her. She frequently spoke out against it.*
'Please don't make me a joke. End the interview with what I

With Arthur Miller

believe . . . I don't mind making jokes, but I don't like being
looked at as one. I want to be an artist – an actress with integrity.
My work is the only ground I've ever had to stand on. I seem to
have a whole superstructure with no foundation – but I'm
working on the foundation.'

Unlike Marilyn, Arthur Miller was a fan of both Bus Stop *and*
The Prince and the Showgirl.
'I think Arthur secretly likes dumb blondes. Never had one before
me. Some help he is.'

Following the success of Some Like It Hot *in which she had given an unsurpassable performance as the perfect dumb blonde . . .*
'That's it! I'm stuck. I'm a dumb blonde for ever now. I've ruined everything for myself!'

In Let's Make Love

During the shooting of Let's Make Love, *Marilyn kept a diary, in which she made the following note:*
'What am I afraid of? Why am I so afraid? Do I think I can't act? I know I can act but I am afraid. I am afraid and I should not be and I must not be. Fuck!'

With John Huston and Arthur Miller on the set of The Misfits

About the script of Let's Make Love:
'It's ridiculous. All my movies are ridiculous. At least with Fox.
That's why I want to get finished, and then do exactly
what I want!'

About her role in The Misfits *Marilyn said:*
'I convince them by throwing a fit, not by explaining why it's
wrong. I guess they thought I was too dumb to explain anything,
so I have a fit. A screaming, crazy fit. I mean nuts. And to think,
Arthur did this to me. He was supposed to be writing this for me.
He could have written me *anything* and he comes up with *this*. If
that's what he thinks of me, well, then I'm not for him and he's
not for me.
   'Arthur knows how I feel about colour. I'm gonna look awful.
Gee, it's depressing enough as it is. Who would pay to see that?
You would think with all the money they're paying for the stars
and all, they'd make it in colour. Then, at least, it'd look pretty.
They're so stupid. Nobody would be in this movie, nobody,
if it wasn't for the money . . .
   'Arthur said it's *his* movie. I don't think he even wants me in it.
It's all over. We have to stay with each other because it would be
bad for the film if we split up now. I don't know how long I can
put up with this. I think that Arthur's been complaining to Huston
about everything he thinks is wrong with me, that I'm mental or
something. And that's why Huston treats me like an idiot with his
"dear this" and "dear that." Why doesn't he treat me like a normal

actress? I wish he'd give me the same attention that he gives to
those bloody gambling machines in Reno because that's what he
really enjoys.

'It's their film. It's about cowboys and horses, they don't need
anything else. As for me, they don't need me at all, not as an
actress. Only for the money. To be able to put my name on the
film. To seduce people to come in and spend their money, to see
another sex film about a dumb blonde. Well it's not going to be
that easy this time!'

During the shooting of Something's Got To Give, *in which she played
opposite Dean Martin, Marilyn Monroe was fired after all kinds of*

*difficulties with the studio. In her own opinion, the difficulties only arose
because she was ill.*

'A struggle with shyness is in every actor more than anyone can
imagine . . . I'm one of the world's most self-conscious people.
I really have to struggle . . . An actor is not a machine, no matter
how much they want to say you are.

   'The executives can get colds and stay home forever and phone
it in; but how dare you, the actor, get a cold or virus . . . I wish
they had to act a comedy with a temperature and a virus infection.
I'm not an actress who appears at the studio just for the purpose
of discipline. This doesn't have anything to do with art . . . this is
supposed to be an art form, not just a manufacturing
establishment.'

With Dean Martin in
Something's Got To Give

men

'A career is a wonderful thing, but you can't snuggle up to it on a cold night.'

Shortly before her death, Marilyn Monroe met the Mexican scriptwriter, José Bolanos. He was one of her last lovers.
'He isn't at all handsome. None of my men are. But he has unbelievable manners. And he's the greatest lover in the whole wide world! I hear he makes some of the worst movies in Mexico! Silly romances. But what do I care? Everything else he does is incredible.'

'He asked me to marry him. I can't believe it. I don't know what to say. I mean . . . well, we haven't really talked about it, what

With Jose Balanos

José thinks of my career, where he wants to live. He's even more jealous than Joe. He might want me to get out of movies, too. Wouldn't that be something? And what if I had to live in Mexico? . . . What am I going to do? I love him.'

'If it could have only worked out [with Joe] . . . Why, why didn't it? It's insane . . . two people who love each other and won't get married. Maybe if I wait, Joe'll . . . but if he doesn't, then José might leave . . . and there I am again, with zero. And getting older every day . . .'

'Joe doesn't think any man can love me except him. He's my best friend in the world. I don't want to lose him. I don't want to lose José. I don't want to lose anyone. Oh, help me, somebody . . .'

'It's better to be unhappy alone than unhappy with someone – so far.'

'You know, they talk a lot about animal magnetism. I think Marlon Brando has it without even doing anything. But the most interesting thing about Marlon is his sensitivity. He's really trying to discover himself. He wants to know what's behind everything . . . even while he's talking to you. When he acts on a stage, he's constantly searching. I don't know if he's trying to find himself or

With Marlon Brando

the person he's talking to, but he's always searching. He moves
magnificently. You don't think of him walking, because he moves
like a dancer. I think he's trying to understand everything that
exists. It's unusual . . . especially in a young man.'

*After she'd been to bed with Marlon Brando, she said to Milton Greene
the next day:*
'I don't know if I do it the right way . . . '

Marilyn Monroe was once asked what she didn't like about men:
'Nothing that I can think of.'

*Marilyn had heard that Montgomery Clift was a homosexual, but the
notion of a man sleeping with another man struck Marilyn as incredibly
weird. She knew he was good friends with Elizabeth Taylor.*
'Monty needs a woman to love him. Just like I need someone . . .
He could have any girl in the world . . . I bet he sleeps with
Elizabeth. I bet he does. Why her?'

*Marilyn Monroe tried to seduce Clift, but all he did was to tell her she had
a most incredible ass – and then he left . . .*
'I give up. I tried. Boy, I tried. You know, I kinda doubt that he
does anything with Elizabeth Taylor either. I think I was wrong
about that. He's a mess . . . But I still love him.'

*Via Joe Schenck, Marilyn Monroe came into contact with Harry Cohn, a
studio boss at Columbia. He let her make one film,* Ladies of the Chorus.
'Joe [Schenck] was like Clark Gable by comparison. Mr Cohn
wasn't even the kind who said hello first. He just told you to get in
bed. For him, women were slaves.'

With Montgomery Clift

'There's another sort of man I've never liked – the sort that's afraid
of insulting you. They always end up by insulting you worse than
anybody. I much prefer a man to be a wolf and, if he has decided
to make a pass at me, to make it and have it over with.'

'I hope Clark Gable won't hold it against me if I say that I saw him
as my father. I was only a kid, and according to Freud there's no
harm in that, on the contrary. I dreamed that my father looked like
him, or even that he was my father . . . Which reminds me, it's
odd but I never dreamed anyone was my mother.'

'He never got angry with me once, for blowing a line or being
late, or anything. He never raised his voice, lost his temper.
He was a gentleman, the best.'

Harry Cohn

'Men who think that a woman's past love affairs lessen her love for them are usually stupid and weak. A woman can bring a new love to each man she loves, providing there are not too many.'

"There's another sort of man I've never liked — the sort that's afraid of insulting you. They always end up insulting you worse than anybody."

'Any woman who's with John Huston can't help but fall in love with him, at least the first time she's with him. I remember my first audition. You can be completely at ease with him. It was my first big part. I was terribly nervous. I felt that if I could take off my shoes, I would feel better. He said to me: "Please, go ahead." In that scene, I was supposed to be lying on a couch but there was no couch, so I asked if I could lie down on the floor. He said: "Yes." So I did. Then I wanted to play the scene once more . . . I felt I could do it a lot better. He said: "It's not necessary." I said: "Please." He sat down very patiently and I played the whole scene over again. He told me then that he'd given me the part the first time round. It was *The Asphalt Jungle*. I think the most interesting scene in the film was cut out because of the Breen Office. It was because of the angle he'd chosen . . . No, I won't say any more about it . . . it was simply the angle.'

"I didn't mind doing it, but nothing seemed to excite me. It wasn't him. It was me. But he took it personally, and I had to act like it was the thrill of my life."

'Johnny Hyde told me he had discovered Lana Turner, and now he was discovering me, and that I'd go even further. That made me dizzy.

'He was so sweet, but I just couldn't get excited about him as a man. You know, I had all these ideas about tall, dark and handsome, and all that. He wasn't. He had the best clothes in town, but they were like doll's clothes.'

'I didn't mind doing it, but nothing seemed to excite me. It wasn't him. It was me. But he took it personally, and I had to act like it was the thrill of my life. I wish it had been. Johnny was good,

With John Huston and Clark Gable

With Clark Gable

really good, to me. He even wanted to get married. But after Jim [Dougherty] I just didn't want to get married unless I was head over heels in love. This wasn't it.'

'I like animals. If you talk to a dog or a cat it doesn't tell you to shut up.'

On December 31, 1955, Marilyn Monroe signed her last contract with Fox. In that contract, she expressed her preference for the following directors (in alphabetical order):

'George Cukor, John Ford, Alfred Hitchcock, John Huston, Elia Kazan, David Lean, Joshua Logan, Joseph Mankiewicz, Vincente Minnelli, Carol Reed, Vittorio de Sica, George Stevens, Lee Strasberg, Billy Wilder, William Wyler and Fred Zinneman.'

With Johnny Hyde

'I could never be attracted to a man who had perfect teeth. A man with perfect teeth always alienated me. I don't know what it is but it has something to do with the kind of men I have known with perfect teeth. They weren't so perfect elsewhere.'

Marilyn Monroe said that JFK always laid his hand on her thigh. Once at a dinner, his hand, which was under the table, went further and further until he realised that she wasn't wearing any panties. He pulled his hand back quickly and blushed . . .
'He hadn't counted on going that far.

   'I bet he doesn't put his hand up Jacqueline's dress. I bet no one does. Is she ever stiff!

   'I feel sorry for them. Locked into a marriage I bet neither of them likes. I can tell he's not in love. Not with her. Well, maybe she likes it. Maybe it's nice being the First Lady. I'll never know.'

'Well he doesn't *look* like a President. He's too young.'

'There was like a hush over the whole place when I came on to sing "Happy Birthday" – like if I had been wearing a slip I would have thought it was showing or something. I thought, Oh, my gosh, what if no sound comes out!'

'I like Bobby, but not physically.'

Marilyn Monroe said to Robert Slatzer, sometime in the middle of July, 1962:
'Bobby Kennedy promised to marry me. What do you think of that?'

When Nikita Khrushchev visited Los Angeles, Marilyn was invited to a banquet in his honour.
'He was fat and ugly and had warts on his face and he growled. Who would want to be a Communist with a president like that! I could tell Khrushchev liked me. He smiled more when he was introduced to me than for anybody else at the whole banquet. And everybody else was there. He squeezed my hand so long and so

hard that I thought he would break it. I guess it was better than having to kiss him.'

'I just find Jerry Lewis so sexy. You know, I can't understand it, but that's how it is. Maybe it's got something to do with his vitality. I think he's got a very nice face. I think he only makes funny faces because that's what people expect. Every time he and Dean Martin see me, they start howling and falling about all over the place, and I love them for it. I met Jerry once at a radio show. It was a rehearsal. He wished me luck and told me that the most important thing for me was not to be too nervous. I think he felt that. What counts isn't what he said to me, but how sincere he was.'

With Dean Martin and Jerry Lewis at the Redbook Awards, 1953

'Despite his rough and ready ways, Robert Mitchum is probably one of the most sensitive people deep down. I knew him on location for *River of No Return*. We were in Canada for a month and a half. There's so much irony in everything he says. You never

With Robert Mitchum

lose sight of the truth with him, nor of how things really are. He never dodges an issue. He shocks a lot of people, but what he says is the truth. I think he could be a poet.'

'The chief drawback with men is that they are too talkative. I don't mean intellectual men who are full of ideas and information about life. It's always a delight to hear such men talk because they are not talking boastfully. The over-talkative men who bore me are the ones who talk about themselves. Sometimes they confine themselves to plain uninterrupted boasting. They'll sit for an hour telling you how smart they are and how stupid everybody else around them is. Sometimes they don't even boast but give you an inside on what they like to eat and where they've been in the last five years.'

'Doesn't Yves look like Joe? I love his voice. He's so sexy. Wow!

'And Simone. Gosh, she's smart. How can he keep up with her? Oh, I guess he can, when they're speaking French. I'm going to learn French. It sounds like more fun than English . . .

'Simone's not pretty, and she's older than he is. What did she do to get him? I bet he married her so she'd help him become a *big* movie star. That had to be it. For his career . . . Well, I can't blame him. I mean, it's so hard in movies. You've gotta have connections. Anyway, she's really nice. I can tell he looks up to her. She's lucky.'

Marilyn Monroe made a rather desperate attempt to get Montand to commit himself to her. She booked a hotel room, where she wanted to meet him.

'He tried to be nice. He kissed me and all. But he said the idea of his leaving Simone was . . . ridiculous. That's what he said . . . ridiculous. He said he hoped I enjoyed myself with him and he told me what a "nice time" he had had. I was in love and he was just having a "nice time". The last thing he said was that Arthur and I should come visit him and Simone in France. Wouldn't that be something . . . Why did I fall for him? Oh, why? I think it was when she got the Oscar. I was so jealous. I wanted to say, "You've got the Oscar, but I've got Yves." Now you know they're gonna be sitting in Paris and laughing their heads off at me.'

'We did it! We did it! It was so natural, like we were made for each other. He's a man – tender, sweet, and kind . . .

'I don't think I'm the woman for Arthur. He needs an intellectual, somebody he can talk to. He needs someone like Simone . . . and Yves needs me. I don't think Arthur would care. But Simone . . . I don't know . . . I hope, I hope . . . '

'I find Jawahalal Nehru very attractive. I've only seen him in pictures. He always catches your eye. I can't describe him. You have to admire him for what he stands for, for what he is. He's such an outstanding man . . . he has no limits. He's a thinking

With Yves Montand and Frankie Vaughan

man. What he's trying to do, I admire him a lot for that. I'd love to meet him.'

'The truth is I've never fooled anyone. I've let men sometimes fool themselves. Men sometimes didn't bother to find out who and what I was. Instead they would invent a character for me. I wouldn't argue with them. They were obviously loving somebody I wasn't. When they found this out, they would blame me for disillusioning them – and fooling them.'

"The most unsatisfactory men are those who pride themselves on their virility and regard sex as if it were some form of athletics in which you win cups."

After her divorce from DiMaggio, Marilyn Monroe lived with Frank Sinatra. He didn't ask her to walk around naked when his friends were around, but on one occasion, it happened anyway . . .
'He hit the roof. Frankie slammed his drink down so hard he broke the glass. He yanked me aside and ordered me to get my "fat ass" back upstairs. How dare I embarrass him in front of his friends? When I tried to tell him that I thought his friends would like me more than their stupid cards, I sobered up pretty fast. He looked like he was going to kill me on the spot. I ran back to the bedroom and cried for hours. Here was Frankie being so nice to me, and I let him down . . .

'No one in the whole world's sweeter than Frankie. When he came back later and kissed me on the cheek, that made me feel like a million. From then on I *always* dressed up for him. Whether or not anyone was coming over.'

Marilyn Monroe got the idea that she wanted to marry Frank Sinatra.
'He's almost ready!'

'Joe'll never marry me again. Never. He loves me but that's it. We can't agree about the movies . . . Frankie wouldn't expect me to be a housewife. We can both have our careers. It'll be perfect . . . I hope.

'Let me be lucky . . . just once.'

But her plans didn't work out.
'I can't tie him down, not Frankie, but I'll always love him . . . '

Marilyn enjoyed nothing more than a night on the town. Frank Sinatra,
however, did not indulge her enthusiasm . . .
'He always kept me in the bedroom.'

Sidney Skasky was a famous Hollywood columnist in the 1950's.
'Sidney is one of the most interesting people to talk to I know. It
may seem strange, but I can spend an hour and a half with him and
it seems like ten minutes. I'm fond of Sidney. When no-one paid
any attention to me, he'd say to me: "You'll be one of the brightest

Frank Sinatra

stars in Hollywood.'' I didn't even have any work. I wasn't eating.
And he was saying these incredible things. You know . . . like:
''You don't believe it, but you'll do this and that.'' I met him the
first time I was leaving the Fox offices. I didn't even have any
work at the time, but I'd drop in at the studio to try and land a
part. He said to me: ''For a girl I never see on a screen, I see more
photos of you than of anyone else. When are you going to make
a picture?'' I said: ''When I get work.'' That's how we became
friends. He had such trust in me. After that, I had occasional long
talks with him. I always felt I could trust him. I felt I could tell him
everything. He probably wouldn't like me to say that he's the
fatherly type, so I won't. But he's sweet and I like him very
much.'

'The most unsatisfactory men are those who pride themselves on
their virility and regard sex as if it were some form of athletics at
which you win cups. It is a woman's spirit and mood a man has to
stimulate in order to make sex interesting. The real lover is the
man who can thrill you by just touching your head or smiling into
your eyes or by just staring into space.'

Michael Tjechow was one of her drama coaches.
'First of all, he's a rare human being. And a great artist . . . I don't
know which term to use first. He's the nephew of Anton
Tchekov, but he himself is one of the greatest artists of our time.
He's a magnificent actor. Years ago, he was with the Moscow Arts
Theatre. There's one very noble thing about him . . . recently, he
wrote a book and put in it everything he's learned about himself as
an artist, a writer and a director. It's for young actors and it's called
To the Actor. What he's learned, he wants to dedicate to the young
. . . I studied with him, in his class, and I hope to continue to do
so. For a serious person, he has a great sense of humour.
I like him.'

Marilyn's opinion of Billy Wilder, director of Some Like It Hot, *was
not enthusiastic.*
'He's not a director, he's a dictator.'

l o o k s

'Nowadays, there seems to be a vogue for women with twenty-twenty-twenty figures. In the high-style magazines you see models with their hipbones sticking out if nothing else. But I'm a woman, and the longer I am one, the more I enjoy it. And since I *have* to be a woman, I'm glad I'm me. I've been asked, "Do you mind living in a man's world?" I always answer, "Not as long as I can be a woman in it." '

'People are used to looking at me as if I were a kind of mirror instead of a person. They don't see me, they see their own hidden thoughts and then they whitewash themselves by claiming that I embody those secret thoughts.'

'The Production Code doesn't allow people to show their navels, you know. I don't think even oranges have the right to show theirs.'

Marilyn's eyes never seemed to be completely open in photographs.
'The formation of my lids must make them look heavy or else I'm

thinking of something. Sometimes I'm thinking of men; other times I'm thinking of some man in particular. It's easier to look sexy when you're thinking of some man in particular. As for my mouth being open all the time, I even sleep with it open. I know, because it's open when I wake up. I never consciously think of my mouth, but I do consciously think about what I'm thinking about.'

'For breakfast, I have two raw eggs beaten in a glass of hot milk. I never eat dessert. My nail polish is transparent. I never wear stockings or underclothes because I think it's important to breathe freely. I wash my hair every day and I'm always brushing it. Every morning I walk across my apartment rolling an empty soda bottle between my ankles, in order to preserve my balance.'

'I've never deliberately done anything about the way I walk. I just walk to get there. I wasn't even deliberate about it in the picture *Niagara*, where people said that I walked wiggly and wobbly. I don't know what they mean. I just walk. I've never wiggled deliberately in my life, but all my life I've had trouble with people who say that I do wiggle deliberately. In high school the other girls would ask me, "Why do you walk down the hall *that* way?" I guess the boys must have been watching me and it made the other girls mad – but I said, "I don't know what you mean. I learned to walk when I was ten months old and I've been walking this way ever since." '

'I don't get what they mean by "horizontal walk". Naturally I know what walking means – anybody knows that – and horizontal means not vertical. So what?'

About her audition for the last Marx Brothers film, Love Happy:
'There were three girls there, and Groucho had us each walk away from him. I was the only one he asked to do it twice. Then he whispered in my ear, "You have the prettiest ass in the business."

On the set of Niagara

I'm sure he meant it in the nicest way. I was only supposed to walk
in the movie, but Groucho said he would write some special lines
just for me.'

'I like to wear chic clothes or no clothes at all. Something in
between does not please me at all.'

'Be careful when you give out my hip measurement as 34. Make it
clear that those are my upper hips. My lower hips measure 37.'

With Graucho Marxs in Love
Happy

'The censor's office kills practically everything taken of me – and
what the censor passes the studio retouches. They spend a lot of
time worrying whether a girl has a cleavage or not. It seems to me
they ought to worry if she doesn't have any.'

A journalist asked her if it had ever been suggested that her breasts
weren't real.
'Naturally, it was another actress who accused me. My answer
to that is, quote: Those who know me better know better.
That's all. Unquote.'

Almost everyone thinks that Marilyn Monroe made this comment when
she performed for the soldiers in Korea, but:
'It was at Camp Pendleton, California. They wanted me to
say a few words, so I said, "You fellows down there are always

whistling at sweater girls. Well, take away their sweaters and
what have you got?'' For some reason it seemed to kill them.
They screamed and yelled.'

When Marilyn was lying on the operating table, already under narcosis,
waiting to have her appendix removed, the surgeons found a note taped
to her abdomen:
'Please take only what you *have* to. And please, please,
no major scars.'

Recovering from her appendix operation

'My ass is way too big. They tell me men like it like that. Crazy huh?'

'I don't sunbathe because I like to feel blonde all over.'

To a female journalist who asked if she was a natural blonde:
'There's only one sort of natural blonde on earth: albinos.'

If you really want to feel blonde all over, you have to be blonde all over, so Marilyn Monroe bleached her pubic hair.
'You know, it has to match my hair. With all my white dresses and all, it just wouldn't look nice, to be dark down there. You could see through, you know.'

In 1956, Marilyn Monroe went to England to play opposite Laurence Olivier in The Prince and the Showgirl.
'The English were supposed to be so nice, but they treated me like a freak, a sex freak. All they wanted to know was whether I slept without any clothes on, did I wear underwear, what were my measurements. Gosh, don't they have women in England?'

On Marilyn's thirtieth birthday . . .
'Kinsey says a woman doesn't really begin to live before she's

thirty. That's good news – and it's also positive.'

In one particular scene in Something's Got to Give, *she was supposed
to wear a flesh-coloured swimsuit. But Marilyn had other ideas . . .*
'I decided then and there that the whole movie was as phony
as that "naked suit". So I said to hell with it, and took it off.
You shoulda seen everyone.'

'I don't want to get old. I want to stay like I am. I still can't act . . .
not really. Monty had his looks, but when he lost them, he was
still a great actor. I'm not. I won't fool myself any more. When
my face goes, my body goes, I'll be nothing . . . nothing . . .
all over again.'

weddings & divorces

When she was 15 years old, Marilyn Monroe was sent to live with her aunt, who decided she should get married as soon as possible. Her aunt's choice was the boy-next-door, Jim Dougherty.

'You see, we went to this dance together. Grace had to beg his mother to make him take me. I was fifteen, he was nineteen and already had lots of girlfriends his age. I kind of looked up to him at the time, you know, especially because he had that car. He had been a big shot at the high school, too. I was at the same one, and was a nobody. I even asked a girl I knew to pretend she was a boy and dance with me. I wanted to be sure I knew how, so I wouldn't step on his feet. Well, as soon as we got to the dance and they started playing those slow numbers, the close ones, he didn't seem to mind at all. It was even funny that he was the one who stepped

on my feet. I think he was pretty excited.'

On June 19, 1942, Marilyn and Dougherty were married.

'I had never had a choice. Grace didn't give me any choice. She was leaving town, and maybe she wanted to make sure I would be taken care of. Once I tried to tell her I wasn't in love, and she

With Joe DiMaggio

Jim Dougherty

just snickered, "What do you know about love? You'll be in love after you get married. Just do what I say." So I did. But I never fell in love.'

'Actually our marriage was a sort of friendship with sexual privileges. I found out later that marriages are often no more than that. And that husbands are chiefly good as lovers when they are betraying their wives.'

Dougherty always claimed later that their marriage was a very happy one. The only thing Marilyn Monroe herself had to say about it was:
'It is difficult to remember what I did, or said, or felt during a period when I was dying of boredom. Jim was a good husband, he never hurt me.'

Joe DiMaggio was the only real and enduring love of Marilyn's life.
'We almost didn't meet. I'd heard of Joe DiMaggio but I didn't know much about him. I've never followed baseball . . . I was very tired the night of the date and asked if I could get out of it. But I'd promised. I had visualized him as having slick black hair, wearing flashy sports clothes, with a New York line of patter . . . He had no line at all. No jokes. He was shy and reserved but, at the same time, rather warm and friendly. I noticed that he wasn't eating the food in front of him, that he was looking at me. Then the next thing I noticed was that I wasn't tired anymore. Joe asked me to have dinner with him the next night. I had dinner with him that night, the next night and every night until he had to leave for New York. I haven't dated anyone else.'

'I had thought I was going to meet a loud sporty fellow. Instead I found myself smiling at a reserved gentleman in a gray suit, with a gray tie and a sprinkle of gray in his hair. There were a few blue polka dots in his tie. If I hadn't been told he was some sort of ball player, I would have guessed he was either a steel magnate or a congressman.'

For two years, Joe and Marilyn were 'just friends'. Rumours of a secret marriage were hotly denied.
'I wouldn't want to keep my marriage secret – there wouldn't be

any reason to. Where could Joe and I marry, anyway, that the whole world wouldn't know about . . . ? I'm sure I'm in love with him. I know I like him better than any man I ever met . . .

With Joe DiMaggio

We haven't gotten around to baseball yet, but Joe has great co-ordination.'

"Actually our marriage was a sort of friendship with sexual privileges. I found out later that marriages are often no more than that."

'First of all, one thing about Joe . . . I think he has the grace and beauty of a Michelangelo. He moves like a living statue. I find him

very attractive. Next . . . he's honest, almost childishly so. He can
size up people so quickly, but without ever saying anything. He's
very observant, storing up everything the way a writer would. It
comes naturally to him. He has a silent reserve that I can't do
anything about but wish I understood better. I don't know how to
explain it. It gives him magnetism. I also want to tell you . . . he
has a great heart. I think that's wonderful.'

After their wedding, Joe and Marilyn had a two-week honeymoon.
Joe, it should be noted, was a notorious television addict . . .
'There wasn't a television set in the cabin. Joe and I talked a lot.
We really got to know each other.'

'In the days of the silent movies, Joe and I would have made
a great couple.'

The marriage fell apart after nine months.
'He didn't like the women I played. He said they were sluts.
He didn't like the actors kissing me. He didn't like my costumes.
He didn't like anything about my movies . . . And he *hated* all my
clothes. He said they were too tight and they attracted the wrong
kind of attention. When I told him I had to dress like I did, that it
was part of my job, he just said I should quit. "I'll take care of
you," he said. "Show business isn't any business for a girl like
you." Joe said when he was a baseball star, he got whatever he
wanted, but there I was, a movie star, and the Hollywood people
just pushed me around. He wanted me out.'

Although she was in the habit of not wearing panties, the famous subway
grating scene in The Seven Year Itch *revealed to the world that Marilyn*
wore white. Her co-star, Tom Ewell, loved it. So did the public. But Joe
didn't, and Marilyn blamed the scene for their subsequent divorce.
'It was that skirt thing, you know, when the wind from the
subway blew it up. Gee, imagine if they had let me dress the way I
really do! Wouldn't that have been something . . . ? But what good
is being a sex star if it drives your man away?'

'Even if he read in a gossip column that I had been seen with
so-and-so, he'd give me a terrible time. Maybe I wasn't Mrs
DiMaggio any more, but he still wanted me to be his girl. He
acted like he was still my husband. He wanted us to get back
together, but I wasn't sure. We had lots of good times, but we

On honeymoon in Japan

In The Seven Year Itch

always ended up fighting. I had to fight with everybody at the studio, so why should I fight at home?'

'When I showed up in the divorce court, there were mobs of people there asking me bunches of questions. They asked, "Are you and Joe still friends?" I said, "Yes, but I still don't know anything about baseball." And they all laughed. I don't see what was funny. I'd heard that he was a fine baseball player, but I'd never seen him play.'

Marilyn and Joe DiMaggio were divorced on 5 October, 1954.
'He didn't talk to me. He was cold. He was indifferent to me as a human being and an artist. He didn't want me to have friends of my own. He didn't want me to do my work. He watched television instead of talking to me.'

'Joe distrusted everybody in Hollywood except his buddy Frank
Sinatra. We just lived in two different worlds. He spent all day
in front of the TV set watching some game or another. He went
for days without even speaking to me. He's the moodiest man
I ever met.'

On July 1, 1956, she married Arthur Miller.
'This is the first time I think I've been really in love. Arthur is a
serious man, but he has a wonderful sense of humour. We laugh
and joke a lot. I'm mad about him.'

'Arthur Miller is one of the few contemporary playwrights

who has managed to convey the feeling of our age. In *Death of a
Salesman*, for example, and also in his new play on witch-hunting.
He's also adapted Ibsen. He has the gift in his plays of exciting
people through what he tells them. I know we can still expect him
to do some wonderful things. As a person, he's very attractive.
My favourite play of his was *Death of a Salesman*, but the thing I
loved the best was a book he wrote, *Focus*, on anti-semitism. I
wish he'd write other books. It was a very serious, marvellous
book.'

'Arthur. It was Arthur. He was why I stayed in New York.

He was going to make my life different, better, a lot better . . .

'Arthur was the only "brain" who liked me for me. He wasn't just after something. Those other famous guys out in Hollywood, the ones who were supposed to be smart, well they'd act real nice . . . at first and then, they'd try to do something. They all had one thing on their minds. But not Arthur. He cared. He saw what Hollywood was doing to me. He wouldn't let it happen. He promised. If I was nothing but a dumb blonde, he wouldn't have married me . . . would he?'

sex & life

"How do I know about man's needs for a sex symbol? I'm a girl!!"

Marilyn's first love…
'When he told me "I love you", I felt more fulfilled than if a
thousands critics had told me I was a great actress.
'I tried to understand why life was so different from how it had
been before *him*. Nothing had changed – no hope, no work in
prospect, all doors shut. My problems were still there, but they'd
become like a heap of dust, swept into a corner.
   'There was one thing totally new to me – sex.
   'Sex is very disturbing when it leaves you cold.

When I used to wake up in the morning, after my first marriage, I'd wonder if the whole world was crazy to always be making such a fuss about sex. For me, it was like being told from morning to night about the incredible qualities of scouring powder.

'Then it dawned on me. Other women were different from me. They felt things I'd never known.

How I wished it weren't so . . .

Marilyn claimed to have been raped by a foster parent. The incident, she said, had resulted in her having a baby which had been taken away 'for her own good'. . .

'He had never really talked to me before. It felt good to have someone pay attention to me . . . At first it was nice to be held and kissed. No one ever kissed me. But then . . . then he wouldn't stop. I thought I had to do what he said. Whatever he said. I didn't scream. I didn't do anything. It hurt a lot at first, then I didn't feel anything. I just lay there. I just cried.

'I was afraid Grace'd kill me when I told her. But she didn't get mad at all. She just took me to a doctor. Later on, I went to a hospital, where I had the baby . . . my baby. I was so scared but it was wonderful. It was a little boy. I hugged him and kissed him. I just kept touching him. I couldn't believe this was my baby. I had him in the hospital for a few days. But when it was time for me to leave, the doctor and a nurse came in with Grace. They all looked real strange and said they'd be taking the baby. It was like being kicked in the head. I begged them, "Don't take my baby." But Grace gave me a dirty look and said it was the best thing. She said I was too young to take care of it, that I had caused enough trouble, and to shut up. So they took my baby from me . . . and I never saw him again . . .

'Sex is a baffling thing when it doesn't happen. I used to wake up in the morning, when I was married, and wonder if the whole world was crazy, whooping about sex all the time. It was like hearing all the time that stove polish was the greatest invention on earth."

During the time that Dougherty was at sea, Marilyn Monroe sought diversion in cafés. She notice that in one certain café, women regularly left with the men. Naturally, she was also finally approached by someone.

The man offered her $15 to accompany him to a motel.
'At first I was shocked. I hadn't been around enough to know
what was going on. He had a suit on, so I didn't think he could
hurt me. When I started thinking about a new dress I wanted and
couldn't afford, well ... I was pretty drunk, too ... so I said O.K. I
still wasn't sure what he wanted to do ... He asked me to take off
my clothes. I thought that was a pretty good deal for fifteen
dollars. At the beach I was almost naked ... for nothing.'

About the men that she went along with, she said:
'They would tell me that I was beautiful, wonderful, you name it.
They all acted the same way. I didn't have to say a word. Just take

With Jim Dougherty

my dress off. They just took their own pleasure and ran. I didn't care. I was used to it. I didn't expect anything ...'

She did want him to use a condom.
'He was pretty annoyed. He had to put all his clothes back on and go down and find a drugstore ... He got back real fast!'

For a long time, many thought of Marilyn Monroe as ex-Fox boss Joe Schenck's mistress.
'He had me come over to his house. It was a mansion, I had never been any place like that. He had the greatest food, too. That's when I learned about champagne. What I liked was hearing about all the stars I had seen in the movies. Joe knew them all. He seemed to have this thing about breasts. After dinner, he told me to take my clothes off and he would tell me Hollywood stories. I would just listen to these wonderful tales about John Barrymore, Charlie Chaplin, Valentino, everybody, and Mr Schenck would play with my breasts.'

'What could I say? He didn't want to do much else, since he was
getting old, but sometimes he asked me to kiss him – down there
… I never want to have to do that any more. It would seem like
hours, and nothing would happen, but I was afraid to stop. I felt
like gagging, but if I did, I thought he'd get insulted. Sometimes,
he'd just fall asleep. If he stayed awake, he'd pat my head, like a
puppy, and thank me. All the other girls thought I really had it
made. Ha! I kept going back. At least the food was good.'

*After she married Jim Dougherty, he joined the Marines and was
stationed at a base on Catalina Island.*
'In high school, the guys had started to notice me, but out on
Catalina it was incredible. It was like … like I was a movie star. I
never had thought I was all that great, but, gee, with all these guys
staring and grinning … I liked being told how nice I looked. I
liked it a lot. All my life I was ignored, and now I started looking

at myself for a long time in the mirror just to see what was so great. At first Jim was proud, then he got worried. He didn't trust me … and I guess he was right.'

'Why I was a siren, I hadn't the faintest idea. There were no thoughts of sex in my head. I didn't want to be kissed, and I didn't dream of being seduced by a duke or a movie star. The truth was that with all my lipstick and mascara and precocious curves, I was as unsensual as a fossil. But I seemed to affect people quite otherwise.'

'People say it's very chic to have separate bedrooms. That way a

Joe Schenck

man can have a place for his fishing equipment and guns as well as for sleeping, and a woman can have a fluffy, ruffly place with rows of perfume bottles clinking against each other. But the way I feel, they ought to share the same bedroom. With a separate bedroom deal, if you happen to think of something you want to say to the other one, it means you have to go traipsing down the hall, and you may be tired. For that matter, you may forget what you started out to say. Besides, separate bedrooms are lonely. I think people need human warmth even when they're asleep and

unconscious.

'For a man and a wife to live intimately together is no easy thing at best. If it's not just exactly right in every way it's practically impossible. However, I'm still optimistic...

'However, I think TV sets should be taken out of the bedroom ... Everything I say to you I speak from experience. You can make what you want of that.'

'One good kiss deserves another.'

About Natasha Lytess, her drama coach.
'I was so confused back then, I'd let any guy, or girl, do what they wanted if I thought they were my friend. I let Natasha, but that was wrong. She wasn't like a guy. You know, just have a good time and that's that. She got really jealous about the men I saw, everything. She thought she was my husband. She was a great teacher, but that part of it ruined things for us. I got scared of her, had to get away.'

'People have curious attitudes about nudity, just as they have about sex. Nudity and sex are the most commonplace things in the world. Yet people often act as if they were things that existed only on Mars.'

'I wasn't aware of anything sexual in their new liking for me, and there were no sex thoughts in my mind. I didn't think of my body.'

'Sex is a part of nature. I go along with nature ...'

'Who said nights were for sleep ...'

When asked what she wore in bed, Marilyn replied:
'Chanel No. 5.'

'I think femininity and beauty are ageless and can't be faked, and that true glamour – I know the manufacturers aren't going to like this – isn't a factory product. Not real glamour, in any case, which is based upon femininity. Sexuality is only attractive when it's natural and spontaneous.'

'It's easier to look sexy when you are thinking of one man in particular.'

'There are people to whom other people react, and other people who do nothing for people. I react to men, too, but I don't do it because I'm trying to prove that I'm a woman. Personally I react to Marlon Brando. He's a favourite of mine.

   'There are two kinds of reactions. When you see some people you say, "Gee!" When you see other people you say "Ugh!" If that part about my being a symbol of sex is true, it ought to help out at the box office, but I don't want to be commercial about it . . .
'After all, it's a responsibility, too – being a symbol, I mean.'

'Men feel as if they want to spend *all* night with me.'

'Joe's not bad. He can hit home runs. If that's all it takes, we'd still be married. I still love, him, though. He's genuine.'

'Joe just sweeps you off your feet without even trying. But Frankie, he doesn't sweep you, he knocks you over. He goes wild. God, does that guy *love* women.'

'You know, Frankie (Sinatra) and Joe (DiMaggio) have one thing in common . . .'

'When I'm sitting at a table with a man, I don't think much about what I'm eating.'

Marilyn was a great believer in the power of massage ...
'If you get massages, you'll never need another sleeping pill. I'm so-o-o relaxed.'

When asked if she had anything on when posing for the famous calendar shots, Marilyn replied:
'The radio.'

'How can they say we're having a romance? He's married ...'

'I've noticed that men generally leave married women alone and treat them with respect. It's too bad for married women. Men are always ready to respect someone who bores them. And if most married women, even the pretty ones look so dull, it's because they're getting too much respect.'

'I'm very definitely a women and I enjoy it.'

Epitaph:

'Here lies Marilyn. No lies. Only lays.'

films

Scudda Hoo! Scudda Hay!
(Twentieth Century-Fox, 1948)
With June Haver and Lon McCallister.

Marilyn Monroe plays the part of a farmer's daughter. The assistant director said: 'You walk over to June Haver, smile at her and then you say "hello". Then you walk on. Understand?' Unfortunately, the scene was cut from the film.

On the set of Scudda Hoo! Scudda Hay!

Dangerous Years
(Twentieth Century-Fox, 1948)
With William Halop and Anne Todd.
Script: Arnold Belgard. Director: Arthur Pierson.

A melodrama about juvenile delinquency. Marilyn Monroe plays the part of Eva, a waitress in a café where the teenagers hang out.

Ladies of the Chorus
(Columbia, 1948)
With Adele Jergens and Rand Brooks.
Script: Harry Sauber and Joseph Carol. Director: Phil Karlson.

Marilyn Monroe plays a chorus girl who becomes the star of the show. She falls in love with a rich young man, who doesn't know anything about her background. He discovers that she works in a chorus, but they get married anyway. Marilyn sings two songs in the film: *Every Baby Needs a Da Da Daddy* and *Anyone Can Tell I Love You.*

Love Happy
(United Artists – Mary Pickford Presentation, 1950)
With Groucho, Harpo and Chico Marx and Vera-Ellen.
Script: Frank Tashlin and Mac Benoff. From a story by Harpo Marx.
Director: David Miller.

The last Marx Brothers comedy, with too little Groucho. The only memorable scene is that in which Marilyn Monroe goes to see detective Groucho and asks him if he can solve the mystery as to why men are always following her.

'Groucho told me that they needed a girl for this part that could wake up his declining sexual appetites by just walking toward him. Harpo pressed the beeper of his walking stick once and smiled at me. I started to walk in the manner that Groucho wanted me to. "Perfect," Groucho said, and Harpo beeped three times and blew a whistle on his fingers.' – *Marilyn Monroe.*

A Ticket to Tomahawk
(Twentieth Century-Fox, 1950)
With Dan Dailey and Anne Baxter.
Script: Mary Loos and Richard Sale. Director: Richard Sale.

A sharpshooter must try to prevent a train from arriving in Tomahawk on time. Among the passengers on the train are some chorus girls, one of whom is Marilyn Monroe. Of course, the gunman's evil plan is thwarted and on their way to Tomahawk, Marilyn Monroe, Dan Dailey and three girls sing the song *Oh, What a Forward Young Man You Are.*

The Asphalt Jungle
(Metro-Goldwyn-Mayer, 1950)
With Sterling Hayden, Louis Calhern and Sam Jaffe.
Script: Ben Maddow and John Huston. Director: John Huston.

This crime movie has become a classic film. It is the story of a failed robbery and gangsters who betray one another and kill each other off. Marilyn Monroe plays Angela Phinlay, the sweetheart of the influential lawyer/fence Alonzo D. Emmerich, a role played by Louis Calhern. In 1950 it was still impossible for someone to have a lover in a movie, so Emmerich introduces Marilyn Monroe as his niece. *The Asphalt Jungle* is viewed as Marilyn Monroe's breakthrough as an actress.

All About Eve
(Twentieth Century-Fox, 1950)
With Bette Davis, Anne Baxter and George Sanders.
Script: Joseph L. Mankiewicz. Director: Joseph L. Mankiewicz.

A Broadway satire, in which a young, ambitious actress (Anne Baxter) wins the friendship of Broadway star Bette Davis in order to take her place in the spotlight. Marilyn Monroe plays the girlfriend of theatre critic George Sanders, a girl who would do anything to become famous but fails due to her lack of talent.

The Fireball
(Twentieth Century-Fox, 1950)
With Mickey Rooney and Pat O'Brien.
Script: Tay Garnett and Horace McCoy. Director: Tay Garnett.

Roller skating star Mickey Rooney lets fame go to his head and instead of concentrating on his roller skating, he takes off after a number of women, including Marilyn Monroe, who plays a girl named Polly.

Right Cross
(Metro-Goldwyn-Mayer, 1950)
With June Allyson, Dick Powell, Ricardo Montalban and Lionel Barrymore.
Script: Charles Schnee. Director: John Sturges.

Marilyn Monroe's part (her sixth movie that year) was so small that she wasn't even mentioned in the credits. She appears briefly in a nightclub at the table of sports reporter Dick Powell.

Hometown Story
(Metro-Goldwyn-Mayer, 1951)
With Jeffrey Lynn and Alan Hale Jr.
Script: Arthur Pierson. Director: Arthur Pierson.

An ex-politician becomes a journalist and takes on the businessmen who, according to him, control the local politics. Marilyn Monroe plays Miss Martin, one of the newspaper staff.

As Young as You Feel
(Twentieth Century-Fox, 1951)
With Monty Woolley, Thelma Ritter and David Wayne.
Script: Lamar Trotti. Director: Harmon Jones.

A comedy about a man who loses his job because of his age. After all kinds of complications, he gets his job back and proves that age has nothing to do with a person's capabilities. Marilyn Monroe plays Harriet, the secretary of the manager.
   Marilyn Monroe is still playing small roles but the public doesn't care and lets her know through her piles of fan mail.

Love Nest
(Twentieth Century-Fox, 1951)
With June Haver, William Lundigan and Jack Paar.
Script: I.A.L. Diamond. Director: Joseph Newman.

A comedy about a couple who are having financial difficulties and trouble staying happy. Marilyn Monroe plays an old acquaintance of the husband's. Her co-star Jack Paar later wrote in his autobiography: 'I guess I should have been excited, but I found her pretty dull. Marilyn spoke in a breathless way which denoted either passion or asthma. She wore dresses with the necklines so low she looked as though she had jumped into her dress and caught her boot on the shoulder straps . . . She used to carry around books by Marcel Proust, with their titles facing out, although I never saw her read any of them. She was always holding up shooting because she was talking with someone on the phone. Judging from what's happened, though, I guess she had the right number.'

Let's Make It Legal
(Twentieth Century-Fox, 1951)
With Claudette Colbert, Macdonald Carey and Zachary Scott.
Script: F. Hugh Herbert and I.A.L. Diamond. Director: Richard Sale.

A comedy about divorce and jealousy, with Marilyn Monroe as beautiful blonde, Joyce, whose task it is to cause the jealousy.

Clash by Night
(RKO, 1952)
With Barbara Stanwyck, Paul Douglas and Robert Ryan.
Script: Alfred Hayes. Director: Fritz Lang.

A homey little drama, in which Marilyn Monroe works in a fish-canning factory and in which she is particularly noticeable because she doesn't let the experienced actors Stanwyck, Douglas and Ryan steal the show.

We're Not Married
(Twentieth Century-Fox, 1952)
With Ginger Rogers, David Wayne, Mitzi Gaynor and Zsa Zsa Gabor.
Script: Nunnally Johnson. Director: Edmund Goulding.

A film in which five couples discover that they are not married. Marilyn Monroe plays Annabel Norris, who thought she was married to David Wayne. She has just been chosen 'Mrs Mississippi', a title she must relinquish. Immediately, she enters the Miss Mississippi contest, which she wins while her ex-husband and baby watch. The episode ends with them re-marrying.

Don't Bother to Knock
(Twentieth Century-Fox, 1952)
With Richard Widmark.
Script: Daniel Taradash. Director: Roy Baker.

Marilyn Monroe's first starring role, as a psychotic babysitter who convinces herself that a man she has met by accident is her dead fiancé. The film ends with an attempted suicide.

Monkey Business
(Twentieth Century-Fox, 1952)
With Cary Grant, Ginger Rogers and Charles Coburn.
Script: Ben Hecht, Charles Lederer and I.A.L. Diamond. Director: Howard Hawks.

Cary Grant plays a research chemist looking for a formula for a youth-giving medicine. He drinks some of the formula himself by accident and begins acting like a schoolboy. His boss sends his secretary, Marilyn Monroe, out to look for Grant. When she finds him, they begin playing – until the formula's effects wear off.

O. Henry's Full House
(Twentieth Century-Fox, 1952)
Five episodes. The episode in which Marilyn Monroe appears is: *The Cop and the Anthem.*
With Charles Laughton and David Wayne.
Script: Lamar Trotti. Director: Henry Koster.

Charles Laughton plays a hobo who is planning to commit a crime so that he can spend the winter in prison. He begins bothering Marilyn Monroe on the street, but when he realises that she's walking the streets herself to earn her keep, he is the one who flees.

Niagara
(Twentieth Century-Fox, 1953)
With Joseph Cotton, Jean Peters and Casey Adams.
Script: Charles Brackett, Walter Reisch and Richard Breen. Director: Henry Hathaway.

Marilyn Monroe plays Polly, a cheating wife who is planning, together with her lover, to murder her husband. Instead of the husband, it is the lover who dies; then Marilyn is strangled by her husband.

Gentlemen Prefer Blondes
(Twentieth Century-Fox, 1953)
With Jane Russell, Charles Coburn, Elliott Reid and Tommy Noonan.
Script: Charles Lederer. From the musical by Joseph Fields and Anita Loos, which in its
turn was based on the book by Loos. *Director: Howard Hawks. Musical numbers:
Jack Cole.*

Two comediennes are on a ship on their way to Paris, where one of them will marry a
millionaire. All kinds of complications occur en route, but all turns out well in the
end. Jane Russell, as Dorothy, and Marilyn Monroe, as Lorelei, are unforgettable in
this brilliant comedy.

How to Marry a Millionaire
(Twentieth Century-Fox, 1953)
With Betty Grable, Lauren Bacall, William Powell and David Wayne.
Script: Nunnally Johnson. Director: Jean Negulesco.

An irresistible comedy in which three models share an expensive apartment in New
York in an attempt to catch a millionaire. Marilyn Monroe as the near-sighted Pola,
who refuses to wear glasses in the company of men and therefore gets into all kinds of
dire situations; Betty Grable as Loco and Lauren Bacall as Schatze.

River of No Return
(Twentieth Century-Fox, 1954)
With Robert Mitchum.
Script: Frank Fenton. Director: Otto Preminger.

A Western, in which saloon singer Kay (Marilyn Monroe) ends up on a raft, together with Robert Mitchum and his son, in an attempt to escape the Indians. They succeed and Mitchum and Monroe begin a new life together.

There's No Business Like Show Business
(Twentieth Century-Fox, 1954)
With Ethel Merman, Donald O'Connor, Dan Dailey, Johnnie Ray and Mitzi Gaynor.
Script: Phoebe and Leon Shamray. Director: Walter Lang.

Donald O'Connor, one of The Five Donahues, a show-business family, falls in love with Marilyn Monroe, who works as the hat-check girl, Vicky in a night club where she also performs. Following the predictable complications, The Five Donahues with Marilyn turn into The Six Donahues, and together they perform the title song: *There's No Business like Show Business.* Marilyn Monroe also sings: *After You Get What You Want, You Don't Want It, Heat Wave, Lazy, You'd be Surprised.* All songs by Irving Berlin.

The Seven Year Itch
(Twentieth Century-Fox, 1955)
With Tom Ewell.
Script: Billy Wilder and George Axelrod. From the play by George Axelrod. *Director: Billy Wilder.*

An excellent comedy, in which The Man (Tom Ewell), who is spending the summer alone in his apartment in New York, meets The Girl who has rented an apartment above his. There follows a succession of unforgettable scenes: Marilyn walking up the stairs to her apartment after getting caught up in the fan chord; Marilyn saying that she always keeps her panties in the refrigerator in the summertime; Marilyn dipping her potato chips in champagne and Marilyn, trying to cool off on top of a subway air-vent – probably the most famous scene in movie history.

Bus Stop
(Twentieth Century-Fox, 1956)
With Don Murray.
Script: George Axelrod. Director: Joshua Logan.

Don Murray plays a young, inexperienced rodeo cowboy, who ends up one night in the Blue Dragon Café in Phoenix. Cherie (Marilyn Monroe) is performing there, with little success. The clients don't pay any attention to her act and continue to talk until Murray makes them stop. Murray falls in love and tells Cherie that he is going to marry her. And, after a lot of resistance from Marilyn, he does. Marilyn Monroe sings *That Old Black Magic*.

The Prince and the Showgirl
(Warner Bros – Marilyn Monroe Productions, 1957)
With Laurence Olivier and Sybil Thorndike.
Script: Terence Rattigan. Director: Laurence Olivier.

The Prince Regent of Carpathia, Grand Duke Charles (Laurence Olivier), is in
London in 1911 for the crowning of King George V. In London, he meets the
American actress, Elsie Marina (Marilyn Monroe). The Prince Regent falls in love,
but Marilyn waves him off, only to discover that she has fallen in love with him.
Now, Olivier is the one who keeps his distance. The Prince Regent eventually returns
to Carpathia but promises to come back and marry Marilyn and she promises to wait
for him.

Some Like It Hot
(United Artists-Mirisch Company, 1959)
With Jack Lemmon, Tony Curtis, George Raft and Joe E. Brown.
Script: Billy Wilder and I.A.L. Diamond. Director: Billy Wilder.

One of her most popular films, *Some Like It Hot* is an unsurpassed comedy and
without question Marilyn Monroe's crowning achievement. The story: Saxophone
player Tony Curtis and bass player Jack Lemmon have accidentally witnessed the St
Valentine's Day Massacre. They flee and, disguised as women, go to work in a ladies'
orchestra. There they meet Sugar Kane. Curtis falls in love with her while Lemmon
must endure the advances made by millionaire Joe Brown.
Marilyn Monroe sings: *I Wanna Be Loved By You, Running Wild* and *I'm Through with
Love.*

On location for Some Like It
Hot

Let's Make Love
(Twentieth Century-Fox, 1960)
With Yves Montand and guest stars Bing Crosby, Milton Berle and Gene Kelly.
Script: Norman Krasna. Director: George Cukor.

Yves Montand, the millionaire in the story, knows he will be made a fool of in a Broadway show. Instead of becoming angry, he goes to see it and meets the star, Amanda Dell, played by Marilyn Monroe. The show's director thinks that Montand is an auditioning actor and hires him. Montand accepts the part and goes to work, falling in love with Monroe, of course. The outcome is predictable. Marilyn Monroe sings: *My Heart Belongs to Daddy, Let's Make Love, Incurably Romantic* and *Specialisation.*

The Misfits
(United Artists-Seven Arts, 1961)
With Clark Gable, Montgomery Clift, Eli Wallach and Thelma Ritter.
Script: Arthur Miller. Director: John Huston.

This is the film which should have been *Marilyn's* film, if only for the fact that Gable was in it (she dreamt that he was her father). The script was by husband-writer-celebrity Arthur Miller and the director was Huston.

Marilyn Monroe, playing Roslyn Tabor, divorces her husband and ends up with Clark Gable. Gable goes out with a few friends to catch wild horses, which are to be sold for dogfood. Gable shows who's boss by catching a horse, against Monroe's will, and then letting it go again.

'Where are we going?' she says at the end of the film and Gable gives her the only possible answer (which was not in the script): 'Home'.

Something's Got to Give
(Twentieth Century-Fox, 1962)
With Dean Martin, Cyd Charisse and Phil Silvers.
Script: Nunnally Johnson. Director: George Cukor.

A remake of the Cary Grant-Irene Dunne film *My Favorite Wife*. After seven years, a woman returns home from an uninhabited island to discover that her husband has married someone else. Marilyn did a nude scene, and was fired by Fox.

Marilyn
(Twentieth Century-Fox, 1963)
A compilation film.